wild, wild world

SPIDERS
AND OTHER CREEPY-CRAWLIES

Written by
Denny Robson

Illustrated by
James Field

p

This is a Parragon Book
First published in 2001

Parragon
Queen Street House
4 Queen Street
Bath BA1 1HE, UK

Produced by

David West ☥☥ Children's Books
7 Princeton Court
55 Felsham Road
Putney
London SW15 1AZ

British Library Cataloguing-in-Publication Data

A catalogue record for this book is available from
the British Library.

ISBN 0-75254-664-3

Printed in Italy

Designer
Jenny Skelly
Illustrators
James Field
(SGA)
Rob Shone
Cartoonist
Peter Wilks
(SGA)
Editor
James Pickering
Consultant
Steve Parker

CONTENTS

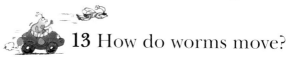

Are spiders insects?

No. Spiders belong to a group called arachnids, which also includes scorpions, mites and ticks. Spiders all have eight legs, one pair more than insects. They have two body parts – a head and an abdomen – and most have eight simple eyes.

Is it true?
Spiders and insects have bones.

No. Instead they all have a hard casing on the outside called an exoskeleton. This protects their soft insides like a suit of armour and gives them their shape. They have to replace this casing with a new one in order to grow.

Wolf spider

4

Amazing! There are creepy-crawlies living just about everywhere in the world, under water, in caves, down deep holes and even on the tops of mountains. Most of the animals in the world are insects. They make up 85% of all known animal species and there are probably millions more waiting to be discovered!

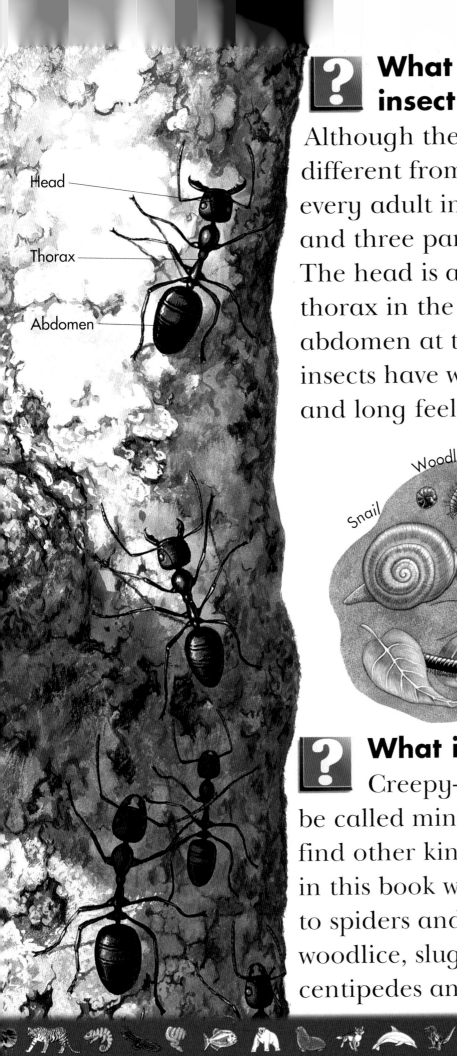

Head

Thorax

Abdomen

? What makes an insect an insect?

Although they may look different from one another, every adult insect has six legs and three parts to its body. The head is at the front, the thorax in the middle and the abdomen at the back. Many insects have wings for flying and long feelers or *antennae*.

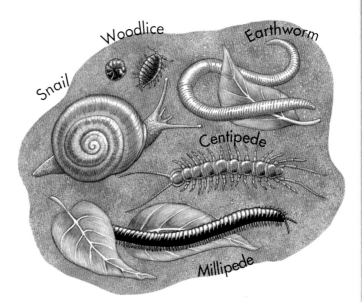

Woodlice

Earthworm

Snail

Centipede

Millipede

? What is a minibeast?

Creepy-crawlies can also be called minibeasts. You will find other kinds of minibeasts in this book which are related to spiders and insects, such as woodlice, slugs, snails, worms, centipedes and millipedes.

Which insect is as heavy as an apple?

The heaviest insect in the world is the African Goliath beetle. It weighs about 110 g and can be 15 cm long. It lives in rotten wood in tropical forests.

Is it true?
Some creepy-crawlies can live for 50 years.

6

Yes. A queen termite may live to this ripe old age. But the life of an adult mayfly may be only a few hours long – just enough time for the mayfly to find a mate.

Goliath beetle

What grows up inside the eggs of other insects?

Fairy flies are actually tiny wasps, some of which have a wing span no bigger than a full-stop! The female can lay up to 20 eggs inside the egg of another insect.

Fairy fly on insect eggs

Amazing! Fleas can jump 150 times their own body length. If humans could do this, we would be able to jump half a kilometre in the air! Fleas are wingless insects which suck blood from birds and mammals.

What is the strongest animal in the world?

Believe it or not, it's an insect. The rhinoceros beetle is able to move 850 times its own weight. Can you imagine trying to carry 850 people the same size as you?

Rhinoceros beetle

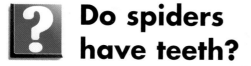

? Do spiders have teeth?

No, but they have fangs for stabbing prey and injecting it with poison and special juices. The victims turn to liquid inside so that the spider can then suck them up like soup!

Indian ornamental tarantula

? Why do spiders spin webs?

Sticky webs can be a home and a trap to catch flying insects. But not all spiders make webs, and not all webs are the same. The ogre-eyed spider makes a web like a net. It hangs down holding the web, waiting to throw it over its prey.

What can see with its tail?

As well as a sting, some scorpions also have light-sensitive cells in their tails. These cells let them know whether it's day or night, even when their heads are underground. Scorpions hunt at night and spend the day hidden in their burrows.

Emperor scorpion

Amazing! The water spider makes its home under the surface of the water. It spins a web like a balloon which it fills with air bubbles. It waits inside until it spots its prey, and then darts out to seize it.

Is it true?
Some spiders eat their webs.

Yes. Orb web spiders eat the old web before they spin a new one. A web may take an hour to spin. The silk is as strong as steel of the same thickness.

Water spider

? What can find its mate over a kilometre away in the dark?

Using its enormous feathery antennae, the male emperor moth can track down the scent of its mate even when she is far away. An insect's antennae are used for touching, smelling and tasting.

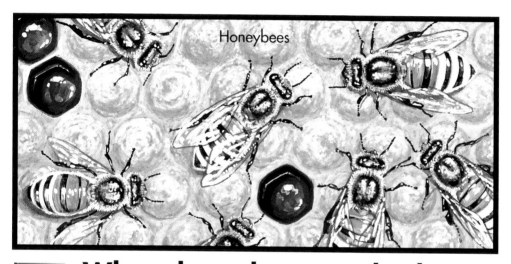

Honeybees

? What does the waggle dance?

When a honeybee finds a good source of nectar, it flies back to the hive and does a special dance. The speed and direction of its movements tell the others where they can find the nectar.

Is it true?
All beetles can fly.

No. Most have wings, but not all can fly. Beetles usually have two sets of wings. The first set is hard and strong, with the flying wings hidden beneath.

10

Eyes of a fly

? Why is it so hard to swat a fly?

An insect's eye is made up of thousands of lenses. This means it sees a very different world from us. It's also much better at sensing any movement nearby.

Emperor moth

Amazing! Dragonflies and some wasps and moths can fly as fast as 50 kph. Butterflies flap their wings 5 – 12 times per second, the hawkmoth 70 times, while some tiny flies can beat their wings 1,000 times each second!

? What is the difference between a centipede and a millipede?

Centipedes and millipedes have long, bendy bodies made up of segments. A millipede has two pairs of legs on each segment, but centipedes have only one pair on each segment. Millipedes are plant-eaters. Centipedes are meat-eaters, hunting at night for tiny creatures which they attack with powerful poisonous jaws.

Snail

Centipede

12

? What travels on one big foot?

Snails and slugs glide slowly along on one long muscular foot, leaving a trail of slime behind them. They prefer damp, dark places and are most active at night.

No. Gardeners like worms. Earthworms feed on dead plants and soil. As they move through the earth they help mix the soil, which is good. Their burrows put air in the soil and help water to drain away.

? How do worms move?

Earthworms live in burrows in the ground. They have no legs, no feet and no skeleton. But their long soft bodies are perfectly shaped to move easily through the earth. They move by stretching and contracting their muscles.

13

Millipede

Earthworms

What is the difference between a moth and a butterfly?

Butterflies are often brightly coloured. They fly during the day and their antennae have rounded ends. Moths have feathery antennae, and fly at night.

Croesus moth

Heliconid butterfly

Which butterfly can fly thousands of kilometres?

The American monarch butterfly lives in the United States and Canada. When autumn approaches, thousands travel south to Florida, California and Mexico – a journey of over 3,000 kilometres.

Peacock butterfly

Is it true?
Butterflies and moths have scales.

Yes. Butterflies and moths have four wings covered with tiny overlapping scales which shimmer in the light. These scales give them their bold patterns and beautiful colours.

Amazing! Before laying eggs, butterflies test food plants with their antennae and tongues to check that the leaves are suitable for their caterpillars. But some also stamp on the leaves, because butterflies, flies and honeybees have taste organs in their feet!

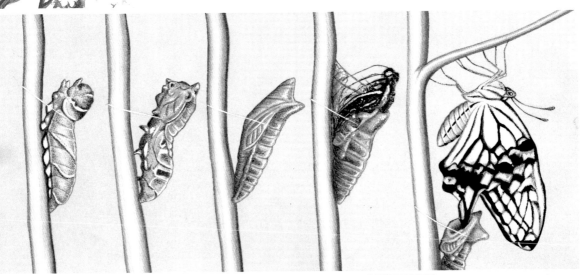

Metamorphosis

How do caterpillars become butterflies?

When a caterpillar is fully grown, it turns into a pupa. Inside the pupa case the caterpillar's body breaks down and gradually becomes a butterfly. This change is called metamorphosis.

Tortoiseshell butterfly

? When is a plant not a plant?

When it's a stick or leaf insect! Stick and leaf insects are the same colour and shape as the twigs and leaves on which they feed. During the day they sit very still. Predators leave them alone because they don't realise that they are insects.

Leaf insect

Stick insect

Eyed hawkmoth

? What frightens off enemies with its 'eyes'?

The eyed hawkmoth raises its front wings to show bold markings which look like large eyes. This fools enemies into thinking the moth is a much bigger animal than it really is.

Amazing! Beetles and woodlice have an armour covering so tough that it is difficult to crush. This protects them from their enemies. Some woodlice and millipedes roll into a ball like a hedgehog when they are threatened.

Woodlouse

? What pretends to be dead?

Click beetles lie on their backs as if they were dead to fool their enemies. Then they suddenly spring up in the air, twist and land on their feet, and run away!

Is it true?
Some spiders can change colour.

Yes. Crab spiders can change colour to match the flowers they hide in. Lots of insects use camouflage to hide from their enemies. Invisible against the petals, the crab spider can pounce on unsuspecting bees, flies and butterflies as they visit the flower.

What uses a lasso to catch its prey?

The Bolas spider gives off a scent that attracts a particular moth. When the moth approaches, the spider swings out a line of silk with a sticky ball at the end. The ball sticks to the moth. The spider then hauls it in for supper.

Bolas spider

Stag beetles

Amazing! Some insects' jaws have become weapons. Beetles have strong biting jaws. The largest belong to the stag beetle. They look like antlers and can be as long as the beetle's body. Beetles are the largest group of animals in the world, with over 300,000 kinds!

? What is well equipped for battle?

Scorpions are protected with tough leathery armour. They also have many weapons – jagged jaws, huge pincers and a poisonous sting in their tail. Some have stings as venomous as a cobra's bite.

 Is it true?
Ants can fire acid at their enemies.

Yes. Wood ants fire a stinging acid from their abdomens. Ants can be dangerous little creatures. They can bite, and then squirt acid into the wound.

? What spits at its prey?

All spiders produce silk, but only about half use silk to make webs or traps to catch prey. Other spiders hunt or pounce on their victims. The spitting spider lives up to its name. It catches prey by shooting sticky poisonous gum at it, fired through its fangs.

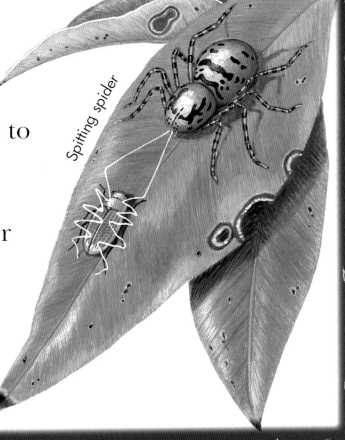

Spitting spider

❓ What uses a trapdoor to catch its prey?

The trapdoor spider builds an underground burrow, lined with silk and covered with a hinged lid. It lifts up the lid just a little, peeps out and waits. When prey approaches, it flips open the trapdoor, leaps out and attacks.

Young dragonfly

Trapdoor spider

❓ What catches its victims with its lip?

Young dragonflies live in ponds and streams. They catch tadpoles and small fish using a special lower lip, which shoots out to stab and hold prey.

Is it true?
Wasps will not attack spiders.

No. The sting of the large spider wasp can paralyse a spider three times its size. The wasp then lays an egg on the spider. When the larva hatches it eats the spider alive.

Amazing! Spider webs come in many shapes and sizes. The purse web spider spins a long, tube-shaped web. The spider waits inside the web until an unsuspecting insect lands on the outside of the web. Then it bites through the silk and catches its prey.

Millipede

? What creeps up on its prey?

The jumping spider stalks its prey like a cat, before suddenly pouncing. Even with eight eyes, most spiders are short-sighted, and rely on hairs on their legs to sense vibrations. But jumping spiders have excellent eyesight.

Jumping spider

? When is an ant not an ant?

When it's a 'jar'. Honeypot ants store nectar and honeydew when there are lots of flowers in bloom. They use some of the workers as 'jars'. They fill them with nectar until they are so fat they cannot move. The ants are 'milked' later when flowers are not so plentiful.

Honeypot ant

22

Is it true?
All mosquitoes suck blood.

No. Only female mosquitoes suck blood. They can't lay their eggs without it. In the hotter parts of the world, biting insects can pass on diseases to humans. Malaria is carried by mosquitoes. It kills over one million people each year.

Mosquito

Amazing! There are insects that eat wool, leather, tobacco, books, blood, carpets – just about anything in the world you can think of. One insect, the male minotaur beetle, presents rabbit droppings to its mate as a tasty treat for her eggs!

❓ What makes a bug a bug?

Bugs are a group of insects which all have a hollow needle-like tube that grows from their mouths. They use this 'beak' to suck up juices. Some live on the sap of plants. Others suck fluids from other insects and small animals.

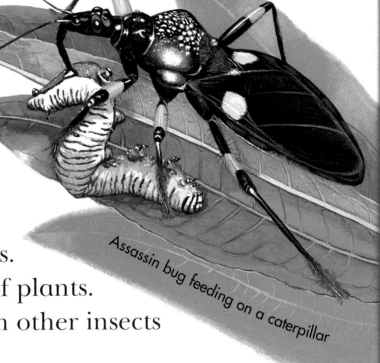

Assassin bug feeding on a caterpillar

❓ Which insect drinks with a straw?

Nearly all butterflies have a long hollow tongue called a proboscis which they use to suck up nectar. They keep their tongues curled up under their heads when they are not drinking.

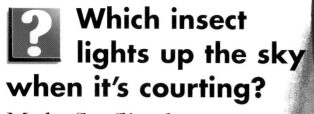

? Which insect lights up the sky when it's courting?

Male fireflies have special chemicals inside their bodies to make flashing light displays while searching for a mate. The females can't fly, but also send out light signals to help the males find them.

Firefly

24

Dancing spiders

Is it true?
Spiders dance to show off.

Yes. Male spiders perform courtship dances in front of female spiders. When they find a mate, male spiders have to be careful. The female may be much larger. The dance helps the male persuade the female to mate with him, instead of eat him.

Why do crickets sing?

Male crickets and grasshoppers 'sing' to attract a mate. They rub their front wings together to make the noise, which is louder in hot weather.

Amazing! Queen ants have wings at first. But after they've flown off and found a mate, they pull or rub their wings off. They no longer need them, because they are going to spend the rest of their lives producing eggs.

Whose mate meets a horrid end?

The mantis eats its prey alive. For the female praying mantis, that includes her mate. She begins to eat the male while they are still mating.

Praying mantis

❓ Who makes a good mum?

A female earwig looks after its eggs and young for several months. It keeps the eggs clean and warm, and feeds the young with food from its own stomach.

❓ What sits on its eggs until they hatch?

Some shield bugs protect their eggs by sitting on them. This keeps them safe from hungry predators. After hatching, they look after their young until they can move about.

Shield bug

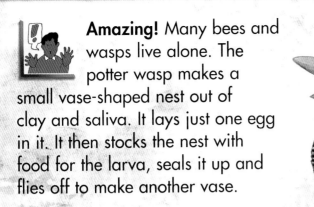

Amazing! Many bees and wasps live alone. The potter wasp makes a small vase-shaped nest out of clay and saliva. It lays just one egg in it. It then stocks the nest with food for the larva, seals it up and flies off to make another vase.

Potter wasp

❓ How do baby scorpions travel?

Unlike spiders, insects and other creepy-crawlies, scorpions give birth to live young. Some of them are cared for by the mother who carries the whole brood on her back. If one of the young falls off, she places her pincers on the ground so that it can climb back up again.

Scorpion and young

27

Is it true?
A queen bee lays up to 3,500 eggs a day.

Yes. Most creepy-crawlies produce large numbers of eggs. This makes sure that at least some survive to adulthood without getting eaten.

? What lives in a tower block?

Termites build air-conditioned mounds that can be six metres tall. These nests contain a maze of tunnels and can be home to millions of termites. Each colony has a king, a queen and soldiers to guard it. In countries with a very wet climate, some termites build mounds with umbrella-shaped tops.

Termite mound

Is it true?
An ant's nest is full of different rooms.

Yes. The nest is made up of many separate chambers, connected by a maze of tunnels. Some rooms are nurseries for the eggs and young, others are food cupboards and some are dustbins.

Queen termite

28

? What makes a nest in a tree?

Weaver ants make nests by pulling leaves together on a branch. They stick the leaf edges together using sticky silk which they gently squeeze from the ant larvae.

Weaver ants

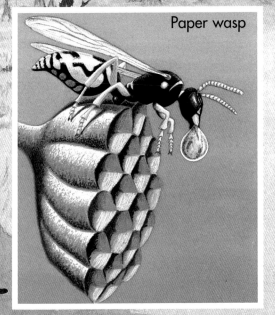

Paper wasp

? What makes a paper nest?

Paper wasps build nests out of thin sheets of paper. They make the paper themselves by scraping wood from dead trees with their jaws and mixing it with saliva.

Amazing! Like ants and termites, honeybees live with thousands of others in colonies. They work together to find food, care for the young and protect the nest. The nest is made from waxy material which they shape into honeycomb. Honeybee nests are very strong and can last for 50 years.

? What helps around the house?

The spiders you see scurrying around your home can be very useful to us. They help get rid of pests, such as flies which carry germs, and there are helpful creepy-crawlies in the garden, too. Hoverflies and ladybirds eat greenfly, and earthworms help improve the soil.

House spider

Dust mite seen through a powerful microscope

Amazing!

Most homes are full of creepy-crawlies, often too small to see without a magnifying glass. Moth larvae eat wool, booklice feed on books, carpet beetles munch carpets, silver fish scuttle under baths, furniture beetles tunnel through furniture, fleas live on cats and dogs, cockroaches lurk behind cookers.

30

Flea

Who has been sleeping in my bed?

Dust mites are smaller than a full stop. They live all over the house, but they particularly like beds. Bed bugs are now quite rare, but in some countries they feed on sleeping people.

Is it true?
Spiders get into the bath by climbing up the drainpipe and through the plug hole.

No. It's more likely that they fall down the bath's slippery sides, while roaming around our houses looking for a mate.

Who has been in the biscuit tin?

Many creepy-crawlies like to live around food. Cheese mites lay their eggs on cheese. Spider beetles eat spices and sauce mixes. An old bag of flour may contain mites, caterpillars and beetles. Guess what the biscuit beetle prefers? Hard dry ones luckily, not jammy dodgers.

Glossary

Abdomen The back part of an insect or arachnid's body.

Antennae A pair of 'feelers' on the head, which help an animal taste, smell and touch.

Arachnid Member of the group of animals which includes spiders, scorpions and mites.

Camouflage Colours, shape or markings of an animal which help it blend into its surroundings so that it is hard to see, and less likely to be attacked by another animal.

Colony A large group of animals living together. Honeybees, ants and termites all live in colonies.

Insect Small animal with three body parts – the head, thorax and abdomen, and three pairs of legs.

Larva The young stage of a hatched insect, which looks different from the adult.

Nectar Sugary liquid produced by plants, and collected by insects. Honeybees use nectar to make honey.

Paralyse To make an animal helpless so that it cannot move.

Predator An animal which hunts another animal for food.

Prey An animal which is hunted by another animal for food.

Pupa A larva enters the pupa stage before turning into an adult insect. A butterfly pupa is called a chrysalis.

Venom Poison.

32

Index